# A New True Book

# EGYPT

### By Karen L. Jacobsen

Flag of Egypt

CHILDRENS PRESS ®

CHICAGO

The Sphinx and the Great Pyramid of Cheops were built by the ancient Egyptians.

Library of Congress Cataloging-in-Publication Data

Jacobsen, Karen.
  Egypt / by Karen Jacobsen.
    p.   cm. — (A New true book)
  Includes index.
  Summary: Examines the geography, history, and modern life of Egypt.
  IBSN 0-516-01184-7
  1. Egypt—Juvenile literature. [1. Egypt.]
I. Title.
DT46.J33   1990
962—dc20

89-25347
CIP
AC

PHOTO CREDITS

AP/Wide World Photos—32

© Cameramann International Ltd.—6 (left), 15 (bottom left), 16 (right), 17 (bottom left), 34 (left), 35 (right), 45 (right)

Chandler Forman—41 (top left)

Virginia Grimes—35 (left)

Reprinted with permission of The New Book of Knowledge, 1989 edition, © Grolier Inc.—7

Historical Pictures Service, Chicago—27

© Jason Lauré—4 (bottom left), 36 (left)

The Metropolitan Museum of Art—40 (right); Museum Excavations and Rogers Fund, 1930—20 (left); Rogers Fund, 1935—20 (right); Purchase 1968, Lila Acheson Wallace Fund, Inc.—40 (left)

Harry and Pat Michalski—33 (left), 41 (bottom left)

North Wind Picture Archives—22 (left), 24 (left)

Photri—© Lance Downing, 4 (bottom right); © Arps, 31 (left); © Richard T. Nowitz, 34 (right)

Melaine Ristich—41 (right)

H. Armstrong Roberts—6 (right), 19 (right); © Alan Bolesta, 26 (right); © R. Scholz, 38

Root Resources—© P.L. Ames, 11 (left)

Shostal Associates/SuperStock International, Inc.—4 (top), 17 (top left and right); © K. Scholz, 8; © Hubertus Kanus, 15 (bottom right); © K. Zwirner, 37 (top left)

Tom Stack & Associates—© Ann & Myron Sutton, Cover; © Wendy Shattil/Bob Rozinski, 16 (bottom left), 42; © C. Benjamin, 28

Tony Stone Worldwide/Click-Chicago—© Laurence Monneret, 13; © Jim Olive, 15 (top right); © Don Smetzer, 15 (top left), 22 (right), 24 (right), 26 (left), 37 (bottom left); © Frank Folwell, 37 (right)

SuperStock International, Inc.—29 (2 photos); © Kurt Scholz, 21

Third Coast Stock Source—© Ted H. Funk, 44 (right); © Philip Krejcarek, 44 (left)

UPI/Bettmann Newsphotos—31 (right)

Valan—© Richard Nowitz, 2, 19 (left), 36 (right), 45 (left); © Michel Bourque, 33 (right)

Horizon Graphics—27

Maps by Len W. Meents—11, 14, 16

Cover — Tourists at the Temple of Abu Simbel, Upper Nile River Valley, Egypt

# TABLE OF CONTENTS

For thousands of years, the Nile River (above) has given life to the land. Six million of the more than fifty million people who live in Egypt live in Cairo (below right).

# EGYPT, THE NATION

"Egypt is the gift of the Nile," said Herodotus, a Greek writer who traveled to Egypt in the 5th century B.C. He saw that without the Nile River, Egypt would be nothing but desert.

Today, as in the past, the Nile is still Egypt's most important natural resource.

More than fifty million people live in Egypt. Most of them live near the Nile River or along the Mediterranean coast.

5

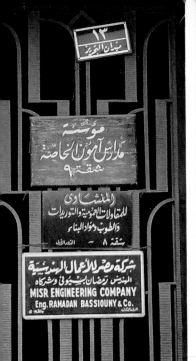

Cairo (above right) is the capital of Egypt. Most signs (left) are in Arabic. English can be found on some signs because so many tourists visit this fascinating country.

The official language of Egypt is Arabic.

Egypt's full name is the Arab Republic of Egypt. Its capital city, Cairo, is one thousand years old. More than six million people live in Cairo.

6

# THE LAND

Egypt is in Africa. It is in the northeast corner of the continent. The Mediterranean Sea marks Egypt's northern border, and the Red Sea forms most of its eastern border.

Egypt is shaped like a square. Most of Egypt is in Africa, but the northeastern corner of Egypt is in Asia.

Two large African nations share borders with Egypt: Libya, in the west, and Sudan, in the south. The small nation of Israel is Egypt's neighbor in the east. Egypt has four land regions: the Nile River Valley, the Western Desert, the Eastern Desert, and the Sinai Peninsula.

Date palms and cucumbers are some of the crops that grow in the Nile Delta.

# THE NILE RIVER VALLEY

The Nile River flows for 960 miles. It runs from south to north and supplies almost all of Egypt's water.

In the north, the Nile passes through a huge triangle of land called the Nile Delta. The Nile Delta is flat and green with cotton plants, sugarcane, and palm trees. For centuries, the floodwaters of the southern Nile have carried rich soil downriver to the delta.

# THE WESTERN DESERT

The Western Desert covers two-thirds of Egypt. It is part of the great Sahara, the desert that stretches across North Africa.

Scattered here and there, are oases where deep underground springs provide water for people, plants, and animals.

This water wheel is at the Al Fayyum Oasis near Cairo.

The Western Desert is not all flat. In the southwest, the Hadabat al Jilf al Kabir plateau rises 3,000 feet above sea level. In the northwest, the huge Qattara Depression drops as much as 436 feet below sea level and contains salt water.

Acacia grove in the Qattara Depression (left). Because the Western Desert stretches into Libya, it is also called the Libyan Desert.

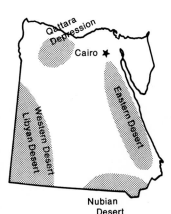

# THE EASTERN DESERT

The Eastern Desert lies between the Nile River and the Red Sea. Parts of it are flat. But, on its eastern edge, the Red Sea Mountains rise to heights of more than 6,000 feet.

In ancient times, heavy rains fell on the mountains. Their waters carved long valleys, called wadis. Today,

The Wadi Galale Road cuts through the mountainous desert in the Sinai Peninsula.

the wadis serve as caravan
routes for people and
animals. There are rich
supplies of oil, minerals, and
stone in the region.          **13**

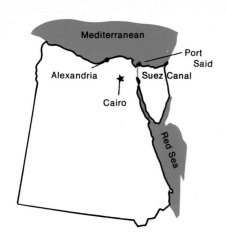

# THE SINAI PENINSULA

The Sinai Peninsula is almost surrounded by water, yet it is a desert area. In the south, there are high mountains. Jabal Katrinah, the highest mountain in Egypt, rises 8,669 feet.

The Suez Canal separates the Sinai Peninsula from mainland Egypt.

Egypt's major seaports are Alexandria, Port Said, and Suez.

Research lab in a cotton factory (top left), soft drink factory (top right), brick factory (left), and a fishing boat (right)

Egyptian workers make
and process food, chemical
products, and appliances.
There is a steel mill at
Helwan, near Cairo.

Cairo and Alexandria are centers for Egypt's world-famous textile industry.

Iron ore, manganese, gold, salt, and oil are found in Egypt. At the Aswan High Dam, the enormous power of the Nile River creates electricity. The Nile is also a waterway for travelers and cargoes.

Young girl weaving a rug (left) and workers building a modern power station at Aswan Dam (right)

Pipes (above) carry the water from the Nile River to farm fields (above left). A young boy uses his donkey (left) to turn the waterwheel that pumps water into the nearby fields.

The Nile provides water to grow crops. Every year, Egyptian farmers lay more pipes and dig more ditches. They irrigate the desert and turn it into farmland. **17**

# ANCIENT EGYPT

The first people lived in Egypt more than 5,000 years ago. The ruler Menes united southern Egypt and northern Egypt into one kingdom.

In ancient Egypt, the pharaoh was a king and a god. The people worshiped the pharaoh. When a pharaoh died, his body was buried with care.

The first tombs were dug into the earth. But later pharaohs built huge, stone pyramids.

The Great Pyramids of Giza were tombs for the pharaohs who once ruled Egypt. The funeral mask of Tutankhamen (left) can be seen in the Egyptian Museum in Cairo.

The pyramids had secret rooms filled with food, furniture, statues, and jewels. The Egyptians believed that the dead pharaoh would use these treasures in his next life.

Paintings on the walls

**19**

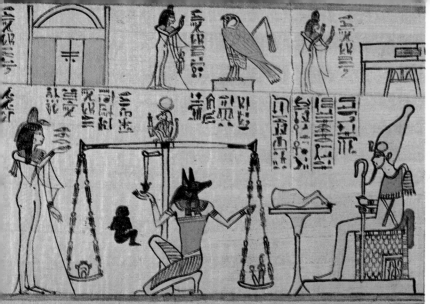 

The papyrus document (left) was found in the tomb of Queen Meryet-amun who died about 1025 B.C. The scarab (right) was carved during the rule of Amenhotep III who lived from 1417 to 1379 B.C.

inside the pyramid showed the life of the pharaoh. Symbols called hieroglyphics told the pharaoh's life story. Each symbol represented a word or an idea.

The Egyptians used hieroglyphics to keep records of everything.

The Temple of Queen Hatshepsut in Thebes, Egypt

Not all of the pharaohs were men. About 1520 B.C., Queen Hatshepsut took over when her husband died. She ruled for twenty years.

Around 1000 B.C., Egypt began to grow weak. One after another, people from other places—Libya, Ethiopia, Assyria, and Persia—invaded Egypt. Each group carried away another part of Egypt's wealth.

In 332 B.C., Alexander the Great of Macedonia took over Egypt. He built the city of Alexandria and made it his capital. After Alexander's

Alexander the Great (left) built Alexandria (right) on the coast of the Mediterranean Sea.

death in 323 B.C., Ptolemy, a
general in Alexander's army,
became king. Members of
Ptolemy's family ruled Egypt
for three hundred years.

Cleopatra was the last
Ptolemy to rule. After her
death, in 30 B.C., Egypt
became a Roman province.

Egypt remained in the
Roman Empire until A.D. 639.
Then, Arab Muslims from
Syria invaded Egypt.

More invasions followed—
first by Turks and then by
Muslims from Tunisia.

Al-Azhar University (above) opened its doors in 969 A.D. It is still a center for Islamic scholars. In 1171, Saladin (left) took over the government of Egypt.

# CAIRO BECOMES THE CAPITAL OF EGYPT

In 969 A.D., Cairo became the new capital city.

In 1171, the Syrians, under General Saladin, invaded Egypt. Saladin ruled Syria and Egypt for twenty years.

In 1187, Saladin's army defeated the army of Christian Crusaders from Europe.

Egypt continued to be invaded by other armies for several hundred years.

In 1798, Napoleon Bonaparte and the French army landed at Alexandria and marched south. But, after three years, Napoleon's army withdrew.

In 1805, the Turks returned. Muhammad Ali, an officer in the Turkish army, seized power in Egypt. Muhammad Ali built factories, roads, and irrigation ditches. He started the growing of cotton and sugarcane.

Children pick worms from cotton (left) and camels carry sugarcane from the fields (right).

Painting (left) shows the first ships passing through the Suez Canal. The canal connects the Mediterranean Sea to the Red Sea.

# SUEZ CANAL

In 1859, the French and Egyptians formed the Suez Canal Company.

It took ten years to build the Suez Canal. During that time, the government of Egypt ran out of money and Egypt had to sell its part of the canal to Great Britain.

**27**

From 1882 until 1922, Egypt was under British control. The British owned the major industries. They opened new seaports and increased trade. They also started a tourist business.

In 1922, the British set up the Kingdom of Egypt. Its king was Fuad I, but he had no power.

In 1936, Fuad's son, Faruk,

In 1902, the British built the first dam at Aswan to control the waters of the Nile.

King Fuad I (far left) was the father of King Faruk (left).

became king. Many Egyptians did not like Faruk or the British control.

In 1941, during World War II, Germany invaded Egypt. But the British and American armies drove the Germans out.

After the war, Palestine, on the Sinai Peninsula, was divided into a Jewish nation and an Arab nation.

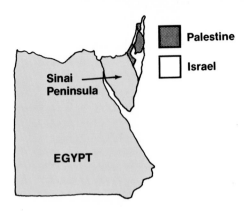

Palestine

Israel

Sinai Peninsula

EGYPT

In 1948, the state of Israel came into being. The Egyptians did not want Israel to exist. They wanted Palestine to be only an Arab state. They attacked Israel. The Israeli army fought back and defeated Egypt.

In 1952, Egyptian army officers took over Egypt's government. King Faruk left.

Egypt became a republic.

In 1954, Gamal Abdel Nasser

Gamal Abdel Nasser (above) took over the Suez Canal (left) in 1956. The Suez Canal was re-opened in 1975.

became prime minister. He made plans to modernize Egypt. In 1956, Nasser seized the Suez Canal.

The Egyptian army continued to attack Israel.

In 1973, the fighting finally stopped. In 1975, Egypt re-opened the Suez Canal.

**31**

President Anwar Sadat (left) and Prime Minister Menachem Begin (right) met with President Jimmy Carter (center) in 1978. Together they worked out a settlement that ended the fighting between Egypt and Israel.

In 1977, Anwar Sadat, the president of Egypt, went to Jerusalem and met with Menachem Begin, the Israeli prime minister. In 1979, they signed a peace treaty. Since then, the two countries have remained at peace with each other.

# THE PEOPLE OF EGYPT

Most Egyptians work in towns and cities. Some work in offices and live in comfortable homes.

But many of the people in Egypt's cities are poor. They live and work in crowded neighborhoods.

Apartment buildings in Alexandria (left) and in Aswan (right)

Village women (left) carry their chickens to market. Hand-painted decorations brighten the home of this farm family (right).

Egypt's country people are called *fellahin*. They live in houses made of sun-dried bricks.

Fellahin men wear trousers and long cotton shirts called *galabiyahs*.

Fellahin women wear jewelry and long, brightly colored cotton dresses.

A group of Bedouin women and children (right) draw water from a well. Rugs and cushions are used inside Bedouin tents (left).

The Bedouins are Egypt's desert herdsmen. Their homes are tents, furnished with rugs and cushions.

Bedouins keep camels, goats, and sheep. They are nomads, always following their herds to new grazing areas. They make their living from the milk and meat of their animals.

Flat bread (left) and a buffet of typical Egyptian dishes (right)

Most Egyptians eat *ful* (fool), a dish made from beans, tomatoes, and spices, every day.

Other favorite foods are flat bread made from corn flour, roasted ears of corn, baked eggplant, and yogurt.

Meat and fish are expensive and rarely served. But lamb dishes are popular.

Coptic Church of St. George (left) and the Mosque of Muhammad Ali (below and below left) are both in Cairo.

# EGYPT TODAY

Most Egyptians are Muslims.
Five times a day, they kneel
in prayer wherever they are.
Fewer than 10 percent of
Egypt's population are Coptic

Christians. They trace their religion back to when Egypt was part of the Roman Empire.

In Egypt, school is free for boys and girls aged six to twelve. In most schools, boys and girls have separate classes.

In secondary school, students study domestic science, technical subjects, or special subjects that will prepare them for college.

There are not enough schools, however. About eight out of ten children go to primary school and only one out of five goes to high school. Many children must work to help their families. Less than half of Egypt's people can read and write.

Highly skilled Egyptian craftsmen made
the gold crown (left) and the silver, gold, and glass
objects (right) more than 3,500 years ago.
These beautiful things are now displayed in museums.

The ancient Egyptians were master painters, jewelry makers, woodworkers, stone sculptors, weavers, and potters. But many of their advanced skills have been forgotten.

Embroidered shoes (above left)
and pottery objects (above) are made
by hand. A simple sidewalk
tent protects this shoemaker (left)
from the sun.

In Egypt today, most people make everyday objects. Shoemakers make sandals. Potters make large, flat-bottomed water jars, called *bellas*. Metalworkers make bowls and pitchers.

41

*Feluccas* carry goods up and down the Nile River.

Along the Nile, sailing is a way of life for many people. Egyptians sail in boats called *dhows* and *feluccas*.

Soccer is Egypt's most popular sport.

Wrestling and boxing have a large audience.

Modern Egyptians play tennis, golf, and basketball. Horse racing is also very popular.

Most Egyptian holidays are religious days. Ramadan is one month long. During that time, Muslims eat no food and drink no water from sunrise to sunset. Moulid El Nabi celebrates the birth of the Prophet Muhammad. On July 23, Egyptians celebrate the anniversary of the 1953 revolution. Sham en Nessim observes the arrival of spring.

# EGYPT'S FUTURE

Egypt is working to
improve the health and
welfare of its people. In many
villages, the government is
building special centers.
Each center has a health
clinic, classrooms, a meeting

hall, a library, a showroom for farm exhibits, and a general store.

In Egypt, there is much that is old. The new village centers will bring many changes. More Egyptians will learn to keep the best of the old ways and to use the best of the new.

# WORDS YOU SHOULD KNOW

**Africa** (AF • rih • ka) — the large continent south of Europe

**ancient** (AIN • shent) — of very great age, from a long time ago

**Asia** (AI • zhah) — the large continent that has the Pacific Ocean on east and Europe on west

**border** (BOR • der) — boundary

**canal** (kah • NAL) — a water channel built by humans

**capital** (KAP • ih • til) — city where the government meets and has its offices

**caravan** (KAIR • ih • van) — a company of people traveling together across the desert

**cargo** (KAR • go) — goods or merchandise carried by a ship

**channel** (CHAN • el) — the bed of a stream or river

**coffin** (KOFF • in) — a box in which a body is buried

**continent** (KAHN • tih • nent) — each of seven large land masses on Earth

**delta** (DELL • tah) — a fan-shaped deposit of soil at the mouth of a river

**depression** (dee • PRESH • un) — land surface that has fallen below surrounding land

**desert** (DEZ • ert) — a hot, dry area usually covered with sand

**Europe** (yoo • rup) — a continent north of Africa and west of Asia

**government** (GUV • ern • ment) — management or control of a town or nation

**herdsmen** (HURDS • men) — men who stay with and take care of groups of animals

**hieroglyphics** (HI • er • oh • GLIFF • iks) — a picture used to mean a word in writing

**independent** (in • dih • PEN • dent) — not controlled by another person or country

**irrigate** (EAR • ih • gate) — to supply water by pipe or ditch system

**Islam** (IZ • lahm) — the Mohammedan religion

**monument** (MON•yoo•ment) —a structure kept as a reminder of a past person or time

**mosque** (MAHSK) —a Muslim temple

**mummy** (MUM•ee) —body wrapped for burial (ancient Egyptian)

**Muslim** (MUZ•lim) —a follower of Mohammed, of the Islamic religion

**oasis** (oh•AY•sis) —a fertile watering place in the desert

**papyrus** (pah•PYE•russ) —a reed from which ancient Egyptians made paper

**peninsula** (pen•IN•soo•lah) —a piece of land almost surrounded by water and connected to a larger body of land

**pharaoh** (FAIR•oh) —in ancient Egypt, the title for the ruler

**pyramid** (PEER•ah•mid) —a structure with four sides that taper to a point on top

**republic** (ree•PUB•lik) —a country with elected leaders

**revolution** (reh•voh•LOO•shun) —a sudden change in government

**route** (ROOT) —a path or course to follow on a journey

**skill** (SKIHL) —great ability

**spring** (SPRING) —an underground water source

**temple** (TEM•pil) —a house of worship

**textile** (TEX•tyle) —woven cloth

**tomb** (TOOM) —burial chamber or building

**treasure** (TREH•zher) —a collection of valuable things

**triangle** (TRY•ang•gul) —three-sided, flat figure

# INDEX

## About the Author

*Karen Jacobsen is a graduate of the University of Connecticut and Syracuse University. She has been a teacher and is a writer. She likes to find out about interesting subjects and then write about them.*